JOKES
FOR
WOMEN ONLY

COLLECTED AND EDITED BY
SUSAN SAVANNAH

and
SHENANDOAH   PRESS

Published
By
Shenandoah Press

ISBN # 0-9613311-3-5
PRINTED
IN
U.S.A.

Women have their faults
Men have only two
Everything they say and
Everything they do.

A nun rushed into the Mother Superior's office and said, "Oh Mother Superior, I've been violated! I'm afraid the new priest, the young one, just had his way with me!" The Mother Superior thought for a moment and then spoke. "Go to the kitchen, my child, and get a fresh lemon." She said, "Cut it in half and suck on it for an hour." "Will that keep me from getting pregnant?" asked the nun. "No," said the Mother Superior, "but it will wipe that silly grin off your face!"

Did you hear that they are going to stop circumcising men?

They discovered they were throwing away the best part.

How does an older woman keep her youth?

By giving him money.

One day a little polar bear cub said to his mother, "Mommy, am I really a polar bear?" "Why, of course you are, dear," she replied. "You live on the North Pole and you swim under the ice to catch fish. You do fun things like playing on the ice floes and running through the snow to catch seals. Of course you're a polar bear. Why do you ask?" "Because," said the little cub, "I'm fucking freezing!"

You can talk to my husband about any subject...

He doesn't understand, but you can talk to him.

If you are afraid of all the deadly diseases out there, but can't seem to give up sex —

Get Married and Taper Off!

A second grade teacher told to her class, "Children, we are going to begin to study sex education. Tonight your first assignment will be to go home and find out what a penis is." Little Tommy goes home and asks his father, "Daddy, what is a penis?" The father pulls down his pants and points proudly saying, "Son, that is a perfect penis." The next day when Tommy gets to school his best friend comes running up to him on the playground. "Tommy," says his friend, "I forgot to find out what a penis is! What's a penis?" Tommy says, "Come on." So they both go into the boys room and Tommy pulls down his pants. He points down and says, "There, if that was a little smaller, it would a perfect penis!"

What's the difference between hard and dark?

It stays dark all night long.

Do you know why it's called sex?

Because it's easier to spell than

Uhhhh... ohhhh... Ahhhhhhhh... AIEEEEE!!

Little Red Riding Hood's grandmother is lying in her bed when the wolf bursts in through her door. "Give me all your money." He snarls, showing his teeth. "Oh, no, you don't," says the grandmother, pulling a pistol out from under the covers. "You're going to eat me, like it says in the book!"

A woman goes to her doctor complaining that she is exhausted all the time. After the test showed nothing, the doctor gets around to asking her how often she has intercourse. "Every Monday, Wednesday and Saturday," she says. The doctor advises her to cut out Wednesday. "I can't," says the woman. "That's the only night I'm home with my husband."

A woman was sitting in the doctor's office when the nurse came in and said, "This isn't a urine sample you brought in. It's apple juice." "I have to make a call," she said. "I packed the other bottle in my son's lunch box."

I found a great new day care center.

It's called COOKIES and CLOROFORM.

A woman goes to the doctor complaining of bad knee pains. After a battery of tests showed nothing, the doctor questions her, "There must be something you're doing that you haven't told me. Can you think of anything that might be doing this to your knees?" "Well," she said a little sheepishly, "my husband and I have sex doggy-style on the floor every night." "That's got to be it," said the M.D. "There are plenty of other positions, you know." "Not if you're going to watch T.V. there ain't," she said.

HUSBAND: Honey, if I died, would you get remarried?

WIFE: Well, I suppose so.

HUSBAND: Would you and he sleep in the same bed?

WIFE: I guess we would.

HUSBAND: Would you make love to him?

WIFE: He would be my husband, dear.

HUSBAND: Would you give him my golf clubs?

WIFE: No. He's left handed.

There are many words you could use to describe men today.

You could say they are charming, strong, caring....

You would be wrong, but you could say them.

My old boyfriend and I weren't compatable.

I'm a virgo and he's an asshole.

The couple had been dating for about six months, but the guy had been afraid to make any sexual advances because of his tiny organ. Finally, he gets up his courage and takes her to a secluded spot in his car. While they are kissing, he opens his zipper and guides her hand onto his penis. "No thanks," the girl says. "You know I don't smoke."

What do you have when you have two little green balls in your hand?

Kermit's undivided attention.

After the women's 100 meter breast stroke, the East German girl filed a complaint with the Olympic committtee. She claimed she came in last because the other girls were cheating. They were using their arms!

A woman goes into a sporting goods store to buy a rifle. "It's for my husband," she tells the clerk.

"Did he tell you what gauge to get?" the clerk asks.

"Are you kidding?" she says. "He doesn't even know I'm going to shoot him!"

A young couple get married, and they've never made love before. On their wedding night the wife is quite anxious to get things going, but the man seems to be having some difficulty. Finally he starts to undress, and when he takes off his pants, she notices that his knees are deeply pockmarked and scarred. So his wife says, "What happened to you?" The man says, "Well, when I was very young, I had the kneesels." He then takes off his socks, and his wife sees that his toes are all mangled and deformed. "I don't understand," she says. "What happened to your feet?" "Well, you see," says the man, "when I was a young boy, I had tolio." So the man takes off his shorts and the woman says, "Don't tell me. Smallcox!"

Marriage is a Three-Ringed Circus

The Engagement Ring

The Wedding Ring

The Suffering

Two bits of advise for the bride-to-be:

One, tell your new husband you have to have one night a week out with the girls, and

Two, don't waste it with the girls.

What's the best thing to come out of a penis when you stroke it?

The wrinkles.

What's one of the worst things about giving a man a blow job?

The view.

How does a real woman hold her liquor?

By the ears!!!

"I'm worried," said the woman to her psychiatrist. "I happened to find my daughter and the little boy next door both naked and examining each other's bodies." "That's not unusual," smiled the psychiatrist. "I wouldn't worry about it." "But I am worried, doctor," insisted the woman, "and so is my daughter's husband!"

Three women were having a drink on the patio of their country club when the door to the mens locker room blew open, exposing a man wearing nothing but a towel over his head. "Well, it's not my husband," said the first woman after looking. "He isn't mine, either," said the second. After a long look, the third woman said, "Why, he isn't even a member!"

My husband has his own method for moving up the corporate ladder.

He calls it the Hindlick Maneuver.

My therapist told me to use some imagination while making love with my husband. I said, "You mean imagine it's good?"

On the way home from the party, the woman said to her husband, "Have I ever told you how handsome and sexy and irresistable to women you are?"

"Why no," said the husband, flattered.

"Then what the hell gave you that idea at the party?" she yelled.

What's the difference between "Oooh!" and "Aaah!"

About three inches.

Do you know what the first obscenity heard on T.V. was?

"Ward, weren't you a little hard on the Beaver last night?"

"Jeeves, remove my dress."

"Yes, mum."

"Jeeves, remove my shoes and stockings."

"Yes, mum."

"Jeeves, remove my bra and panties."

"Yes, mum."

"And Jeeves........the next time I catch you wearing my clothes you're fired."

"Just try to relax, this won't take long," said the gynecologist trying to calm his obviously nervous patient.

"Haven't you ever been examined like this before?" he asked.

"Yeah, sure," she said, "but not by a doctor!"

I once went on a vacation with an absolutely gorgeous guy. As we flew down to Mexico, we couldn't keep our hands off each other. We wanted to fly United, but the flight attendant wouldn't let us.

A couple pull into the driveway after their first date. The guy leans over and gives the girl a long, slow kiss. While he's kissing her, he quietly unzips his pants, takes her hand and puts it on his thing. When she realizes what it is, she screams, jumps out of the car and yells, "I've got just two words for you, Drop Dead!" "And I've got two words for you," the guy shrieks, "LET GO!"

The young man went into the drug store to purchase his first condoms. "How much are they?" he asked the clerk. "8.95, plus tax," was the reply. "Oh, tacks!" said the young man. "I always wondered how they stayed on."

A boy came running into the house and said to his little sister. "Guess what? I found a condom on the patio!" His little sister looked up and said, "What's a patio?"

The cardinal called all the priests of the archdiocese to the cathedral. "I've got some good news and some bad news. The good news is I spoke with God and everything is OK. The bad news is she called from Salt Lake City.

HUSBAND: "Let's go out and have some fun tonight."

WIFE: "OK, but if you get home before I do, leave the front door unlocked."

A woman was complaining to her best friend over brunch. "Everytime my husband climaxes, he lets out an ear-splitting yell." "That doesn't sound all that bad to me," said her friend. "As a matter of fact, that would kind of turn me on." "It would me too" said the first woman, "if it just didn't keep waking me up!"

A woman participating in a survey was asked how she felt about condoms. She said, "Depends on what's in it for me."

The lovemaking was fast and furious.

He was fast and she was furious.

The man came home to find evidence that his wife had been unfaithful. "Was it my friend Steve?" he yelled.

"No," she said.

"Was it my friend Bill?" he asked.

"What?" she shouted. "Don't you think I have any friends of my own?"

My ex-husband had E S P.....
Extremely Small Penis.

A delicate young man went into an army recruiting office. After answering numerous questions, he was finally asked if he was a homosexual. The fellow admitted that he was.

"Gay, huh?" the brawny recruiter growled.

"Do you think you could kill a man?"

"My, yes," the man giggled, "but it would take days and days."

A perfect lover is a guy with a nine inch tongue who can breathe through his ears.

My last lover was so bad....
He should have used AMATEURphalactics!

The newlywed couple asked the desk clerk for a room and told him they had just been married that morning. "Congratulations!" said the desk clerk looking at the bride. 'Would you like the bridal?" "No thanks," said the woman. "I'll just hold him by the ears until he gets the hang of it."

A woman at our church was so infatuated with the priest that one day she chased him 'round and 'round the church and finally grabbed him by the organ.

Why does an elephant have 4 feet?

Cause 8 inches just isn't enough.

After their aerobics class, two friends were changing in the locker room. One noticed that the other was putting on a pair of mens briefs. "Hey," she said, "when did you start wearing men's underwear?" "Ever since my husband found them in my car," she replied.

After her husband passed away, the mortuary called the widow and said that there was some confusion as to whether he was to be buried or cremated. "Let's not take any chances," she said. "Do both."

I've been in love with the same man for 20 years.

If my husband ever finds out, he'll kill me.

My brother-in-law is in danger of losing his license to practice medicine.

He was caught having sex with some of his patients.

It's such a shame.

He was the best veterinarian in town.

My first husband and I never got along. He was an earth sign and I'm a water sign.

Together we made MUD.

HUSBAND: *Honey, I have some good news and some bad news. First, I've decided to run off with Gloria.*

WIFE: *No kidding! What's the bad news?*

A physician was discussing the problem with a retired executive's wife who complained that her husband had lost the sex drive he'd shown during their honeymoon days. "And how old are you?" asked the doctor. "Seventy-two," she said proudly. "And your husband?" He inquired. "He'g going to be eighty-four in May," she said. "I see," said the doctor. "And when did you first notice these symptoms?" "Last night," she answered. "And again this morning!"

Do you know what it means to come home to a man who'll give you a little love, a little affection, a little tenderness?

It means you're in the wrong house.

The friends of the bride were a rowdy bunch — after much deliberation, they decided to give the bride a tape recording of the couple making love as a wedding gift. They accomplished this with a tape recorder under the bride's bed that evening. Before they gave it to the bride, they played the tape. "That's happiness!" they heard her say, "That's happiness!" But her voice sounded funny and they discovered they had the tape on the wrong speed. When they played back the tape at the right speed, they were surprised to hear their friend saying. "That's a penis?! That's a penis?!!!"

I married beneath me.

All women do.

90% of the men

give the other 10% a bad name.

A woman's place is in the house.

(And in the senate)

WOMAN: God, am I homesick!

MAN: But you're at home.

WOMAN: I know. And I'm sick of it!

The doctor came in and sat down. "Your husband is at death's door," he said solemnly. The wife asked, "Can you pull him through?"

A newlywed couple are getting undressed on their wedding night. After taking off his pants, the husband tosses them over to his new bride. "Put those on," he says. His wife looks at him. "What did you say?" "Go ahead, put them on," he says. "Well.... okay." She replies, and she puts the pants on. However, even after tightening the belt, they're still too big for her and they just fall down around her ankles. "I can't wear these," she says. The husband looks at her and says, "Now just remember that. I'm the one who wears the pants in the family and don't you forget it!" The wife immediately slips off her panties and throws them to her husband. "Put those on," she says. "What? What are you talking about?" he asks. "Go ahead," says the bride. "You made me do it, now you go ahead and put those on." "Well, okay," he says, and he starts to put the panties on. They're way too small and he can't even get them up past his thighs. "I can't get into these," he says. The bride looks at him and says, "That's right, and unless your attitude changes, you're not going to either!"

MAN: Honey, has the paperboy come yet?

WOMAN: No, but he's breathing hard.

A little girl came home with her school enrollment card. "Look Mom," she cried. "They gave me an "F" in sex, and I haven't hardly learned about it yet!"

Grandmother and Grandfather have been married for fifty years and they still hold hands.

If they didn't, they'd kill each other!

A man expects his wife to be perfect —

and to understand why he's not.

Two couples were out at a night club when one of the men suddenly lurched backward off his chair and lay motionless on the floor. "One thing about Stan," said the man's wife to the other two, "He knows when to stop."

Waking up with a terrible hangover after the office Christmas party, the man turned to his wife, "I can't remember a thing that happened last night!" he said. "Well," said his wife, "you acted like an ass in front of your boss and he fired you." "HE DID!?" shouted the husband. "After all I've done for him? Well screw him!" "I did," said his wife quietly. "You go back to work on Monday."

"What would you like for your birthday, Tommy?" asked the youngster's parents.

"I wanna watch," said Tommy.

So on the night of his birthday, they let him.

After having quadruplets, the mother named them Adolph, Rudolph, Getoff and Stayoff.

"It's a miracle!" the man shouted, waking up his wife. "When I went to the bathroom, just now, the light came on — even though I hadn't touched the switch. Then, when I was finished, the light went off! All by itself! It's a miracle I tell you!" "It's no miracle," his wife said. "You just pissed in the refrigerator again."

"Remember," the doctor told the elderly couple, "no physical exertion for the mister. And that includes sex. It could kill him."

That night, to avoid temptation, the old man slept downstairs on the couch. But at three a.m., he woke up horney and started for the bedroom. Halfway up, he met his wife. "Oh, honey," he said, "I was just coming up the stairs to die." "And I," she replied, "was just coming down to kill you."

After black Monday the young couple were all but wiped out financially. They had been riding high on the stock market, but now they were faced wtih cutting back on their lifestyle. "We'll have to sell our summer home and the condo in Aspen," he said. "We could sell two of the cars," she offered. "Right," he said. "And we can let the cook go. You'll have to learn to cook." "Wait a minute," she said. "Why not fire the gardener instead, and you can learn how to fuck!"

A husband and wife were fighting about their sex life.

"You never even tell me when you're having an orgasm!" the man yelled.

"How can I?" she shot back. "You're never here!"

My boyfriend told me he wanted some old-fashioned loving....

So I introduced him to my Grandmother.

One woman was telling her friend that since she and her husband had gotten twin beds, her sex life had improved tremendously. "How can that be?" asked the friend. "Well, you see," she said, "his is in New York, and mine's in Connecticut."

Watching her mother as she tried on her new fur coat, the daughter said unhappily, "Mom, do you realize some poor, dumb beast suffered so you could have that coat?" "Her mother looked at her and said, "Don't talk about your father that way."

Every woman should have a man for love, companionship and sympathy.

Preferrably at three different addresses.

A lot of girls are asking if it's wrong to have sex before you're married.....

I say only if it makes you late for the ceremony.

Farmer Jones bought 20 pigs at auction, only to discover that they were all female. He asked his neighbor, farmer Brown, if he could take them to Brown's farm so that they could mate with his male pigs. Brown was happy to oblige.

So Jones loaded his female pigs in his truck, drove to Brown's farm and let them frolic with the male pigs for the rest of the day. That evening, he picked them up and asked Brown, "How will I know if they're pregnant?"

Farmer Brown replied, "Tomorrow morning, if they're grazing — something pigs never do — they're pregnant."

The next morning, farmer Jones looked out his window. The pigs were not grazing, so he loaded them in the truck and took them to farmer Brown's for a second day.

The following morning the pigs still weren't grazing, so he repeated the procedure a third time.

The morning after, feeling very discouraged, he asked his wife, "Honey, I don't have the heart to look. Please tell me what the pigs are doing."

"Well, they're not grazing, but most of them are in the truck and one of them is honking the horn."

A woman and a man, matched by a dating service, began their introduction by phone. After the usual pleasantries and small talk, the guy says, "Well babe, I'm nine inches long and four inches around. Interested?"

"Fascinated," the woman said. "How big is your cock?"

What's the difference between a whale and a husband?

The whale mates for life.

A little boy came home one day and smelled liquor on his Mom's breath. "Mommy," he said, you're wearing Daddy's perfume!"

A young woman went to see a fortune teller. An old gypsy woman dealt the tarot cards and then looking into the crystal ball, she said in a loud voice, "Prepare for widowhood, your husband is about to die a violent death!" After a moment of silence the young woman squinted at the crystal ball and asked the gypsy, "Will I be acquitted?"

If you want to read about love and marriage, you have to buy two separate books.

My husband added some magic to our marriage. He disappeared.

A few months after his parents were divorced, the little boy passed his mom's bedroom and saw her rubbing her body and moaning, "I need a man, I need a man!" Over the next couple of months, he saw her doing this several times. One day he came home from school and heard her moaning. When he looked in her bedroom, he saw a man on top of her. The boy ran into his room, took off his clothes, threw himself on his bed, started rubbing himself and moaning, "I need a bike! I need a bike!"

Why did God create man?

Because a vibrator can't mow the lawn.

How many husbands does it take to change a light bulb?

Six. One to force it with a hammer and five to go out for more bulbs.

Three longtime friends were in their favorite pub having a few beers, when one of them stunned the others by announcing that he was really a woman trapped inside a man's body. He went on to say that he had arranged to have a sex change operation and he hoped they would both understand. Having said that, he got up and walked out.

His two friends sat dumbfounded, staring at each other in disbelief.

Three months later, their friend, who was now a woman, walked into the pub and approached her old pals. They couldn't believe it! She looked great... they would never have recognized her. After a few drinks, they began to question her about some of the more painful aspects of the operation.

"The breast implants must have hurt," one of his pals remarked.

"Not really," she said.

"Cutting off your dick... AND your balls! OOH, that must have been the worst!!" said the other, wincing.

"That was bad," she said, "but not the worse."

"What could be worse than that!?" the two screamed.

"The worst part," she said solemnly, "was when they cut my salary in half.

"I just buried my second husband and I vowed never to marry again," said the woman to her new friend. "That's a shame," said her friend. "What happened to your husbands?" "Well, the first one died from eating poison mushrooms, and the second one was shot to death." "Shot to death!" said her friend. "That's horrible! How did it happen?" The widow shrugged, "He wouldn't eat the mushrooms."

My husband told me that black underwear turns him on.

So I didn't wash his underwear for three months!"

My husband is so cheap, he got his vasectomy done at Sears. Now every time he gets a hard-on, the garage door goes up.

The doctor came out of the operating room to talk with the wife of the patient. "I don't like the looks of your husband," he said. "Neither do I," said the woman, "but he's not home much, and he's great with the kids."

A little girl watched her dad take a shower. She asked him about his testicles. "Those are my apples," he told her. She told her mom what dad had said and her mom asked her, "Did he tell you about the dead limb they're hanging on?"

My ex-husband always used to say, "It's not the size that matters, it's Technique."

Technique aside,

PENETRATION would have been nice!

A man goes to the doctor, and the doctor tells him that he only has twelve hours to live. So he goes home and tells his wife, and she cries and cries. Then she holds him and says, "I'm going to make this the best night of your life." He says, "It's the last." "But it will be the best!" she says. She cooks him his favorite dinner, and opens a bottle of their best champagne. They have a wonderful dinner, and then go straight to bed. They make love, and just as they're about to fall asleep, he taps her on the shoulder and says, "Honey, could we do it again?" So they make love again, and just as she's about to fall asleep he taps her on the shoulder and says, "Sweetheart, could we do that once again?" So they do it again, and just as she's about to fall asleep, he taps her on the shoulder saying, "Darling, could we please do that one more time?" The woman says, "Sure! What do you care? You don't have to get up in the morning!"

Two women were talking. "You know," said one, "for twenty years my husband and I were deliriously happy." "And then what happened?" asked her friend. "Then," she said, "we met."

One of the surest signs that a woman is in love is when she divorces her husband.

As he lay on his deathbed, the man said to his wife, "I can't die without telling you the truth. I cheated on you our whole marriage. All those nights when I told you I was working late, I was with other women. And not just one woman either, there have been dozens." His wife looked at him and calmly said, "Why do you think I gave you the poison?"

If you had perfect pitch, an instinctive sense of harmony and endless musical ideas, what career would your husband urge you to go into?

Keeping house.

When a man and a woman marry, they become one.

The trouble starts when they try to decide which one.

The sex therapist advised the couple to be more spontaneous about sex. "Don't wait for a pre-scheduled time," she counselled. "Make the most of it when the urge hits. Just let all your inhibitions go!" In the next session, she asked the woman how things were progressing. "Fantastic!" said the woman. "Last night during dinner we both felt very amorous. One thing led to another and we ended up having sex right on the table!" "That's great!" said the therapist. "There's only one thing though," added the woman. "I'm afraid we'll never be able to eat at Howard Johnson's again."

HE: Honey, I got a job!

SHE: Great! What's the pay?

HE: Oh, they said they'll pay me what I'm worth.

SHE: What? We can't live on that!

Marriage isn't a word.

It's a sentence.

"It's too hot to wear clothes today," said the man getting out of the shower. "Honey, what do you think the neighbors would say if I mowed the lawn like this?"

"They'd probably say that I married you for your money!" she replied.

The lifeguard told Mrs. Miller to make her young son stop urinating in the pool. "Everyone knows," Mrs. Miller lectured him, "that from time to time, young children will urinate in a pool."

"Oh really?" said the lifeguard, "from the diving board?"

"Mommy, what happens when a car gets too old and banged up to run?" The little girl asked. "Well," her mother said, "someone sells it to your father."

At Sunday School, the teacher asked little Megan, "Do you know where little boys and girls go when they do bad things?"

"Sure," said Megan. "They go out in back of the church yard."

"Mommy, Daddy's on his feet again."

"Be quiet and reload."

"Mommy, how come Daddy's so pale?"

"Shut up and keep digging."

"Mommy, what's an Oedipus complex?"

"Shut up and kiss me."

A woman who had two young boys, had just about all she could take of their foul language. She had tried everything she could think of to get them to stop swearing. Nothing had worked, so from now on she decided to use physical punishment. When the boys came down to breakfast she asked them, "What would you like to eat this morning?" "I'll have the fuckin' Cheerios," said the older one. She swooped down on him and belted him in the mouth. He looked stunned for a moment and then ran into the other room, crying. The woman turned to the younger boy and said, "Now, what would you like for breakfast?" 'Well," he said, "I'm sure as hell not gonna have the fuckin' Cheerios!"

Mrs. Peterson's husband had been missing more than four months. Her friends and relatives didn't know if he had met with foul play or just took off. The city morgue called her one day to identify a body they had found, that might very well be Mr. Peterson. The morgue attendant lifted the sheet to expose a recently dead, but very well endowed corpse. "No," Mrs. Peterson said. "That isn't my husband." She thought for a moment and added. "But some woman certainly lost a very good friend!"

My husband brought home a big tube of K-Y jelly and told me it would make me a happy woman.

He was right!

When he went out of the bedroom, I put some on the doornob, closed the door and he couldn't get back in!!!

"And another thing," the physician yelled at his wife as he slammed the door, "You're a lousy lay!" Later that day, he decided to drive by their house to apologize. When he walked in he found her in bed with another doctor. "What the hell's going on here?" he screamed.

"After what you said this morning," said his wife, "I decided to get a second opinion."

At the funeral, a close friend said to the widow, "You won't find another man like him."

The widow replied, "Who's gonna look?"

My first husband was such an animal that when we went to the zoo, he had to buy two tickets. One to get in and one to get out!

The little girl came running in the house and said, "Mommy, can little girls have babies?" "No," said her mom, "of course not." The little girl ran outside and her mom heard her yell to her friends, "It's OK, we can play that game again!"

If your kids are giving you a headache, follow the directions on the aspirin bottle. Especially the part that says: Keep away from children.

If it's true that girls are inclined to marry men like their fathers, it is understandable why so many mothers cry so much at weddings.

Little Tommy followed his grandfather around all day asking him to make a noise like a frog. Finally, the grandfather asked Tommy why. "Because," Tommy said, "Grandma says when you croak, we're all goin' to California!"

My ex-husband was a C.P.A.

Constant Pain in the Ass.

How do you get your ex-husband out of a tree?

Cut the rope.

How do you stop your ex-husband from drowning?

Take your foot off his head.

A couple were getting dressed to go out when the guy says, "Honey, this shirt collar is so tight, I can hardly breathe. This can't be my shirt. The laundry must have made a mistake." "No, that's your shirt," said the woman. "You just have your head through the button hole."

A man found his wife in bed with another man.

"My God!" he shouted, "what are you doing?!"

His wife looked at her lover and said, "See, I told you he was dumb."

I've developed a new Monday night football drink for my husband.

After three, you kick off.

What's the difference between a mental hospital and marriage?

At a mental hospital, you have to show improvement to get out!

I found out the difference between my husband's family and yogurt.

Yogurt has culture.

A mother took her children to the zoo especially to see the elephants. When they got there, they found that the pens in the elephant exhibit were all empty. "I'm sorry, but it's the mating season," the attendant explained, "and the animals have gone inside their sanctuary for privacy." Over the moans of her disappointed kids, the mother asked, "Do you think they'd come out for peanuts?" The attendant looked at her and said, "Would You?"

In a motel room somewhere in Florida, an elderly pair are committing adultery:

"Kiss me!" the old man said in the heat of passion.

"Kiss you?" says the old woman. "I shouldn't even be doing this!!"

A man came home from work early one day, and found his wife naked and panting on the bed. "Honey," she said, thinking quickly, "I think I'm having a heart attack!" While rushing to call the doctor, he nearly stumbled over his crying four year old, who told him there was a naked man in the closet. He ran to the closet, opened the door, and there was his best friend. "Damn It, Dave," he shouted, "Jill's having a heart attack and here are you scaring the hell out of the kids!"

When does a woman stop masturbating?

After the divorce.

As far as recreation goes, SEX is much better than bowling.....

The balls are lighter....

and you don't have to change your shoes.

Two women were discussing a man that they had just met by the pool. "Well, he's obviously a sincere man," said the one. "Why do you say that?" asked the other. "Because," said the first one, "no one would deliberately pretend to be an asshole."

After the birth of his daughter, the man was brooding in the waiting room. Noticing the dejected new father, the doctor went over to him and asked him why he was down. "Well," said the father, "I didn't really want a girl. I was really hoping for a kid that had... you know... a penis!"

The doctor patted him on the shoulder and said, "Don't worry, in about 18 years, she'll have a fine place to put one."

I think the only reason my husband likes to go fishing so much is that it's the only time he hears someone tell him, "Wow, that's a big one!"

My husband said for his physical, the doctor needed a urine specimen, a stool sample, and a semen specimen.

I said, "Just give them your underwear."

The contractor's daughter asked her mom, "Can I have a baby brother?" "Not for a while yet," said her mother, "Your dad is very busy," They little girl thought awhile and said, "Can't he put more men on the job?"

The gray haired singles bar romeo walked up to a girl of about twenty and gave her the old line,

"Where have you been all my life?"

She took one look at him and said, "For the first half of it, I wasn't even born."

Here are two ways to tell if your husband is too fat: If he steps on the dog's tail.... and it dies. If he starts leaving footprints in your hardwood floors.

After four drinks, my husband turns into a disgusting beast.

After five, I usually pass out.

Sally and Cliff were riding home from the party when Sally asked, "Can you drive with one hand, Cliff?" His eyes lit up and he said, "Sure can, baby!"

"Well then," she said, "wipe your nose before you get snot all over your shirt!"

A good friend of mine says that penises are like fish.

The little ones you throw back.

The big ones you mount!

I was first attracted to my boyfriend at our company picnic.

He won the three legged race.

Alone.

Debby went to see her gynecologist.

"Ever since you fit me with the diaphragm, I've been urinating purple," she told him.

"That is strange," said the doctor. "What kind of jelly are you using?"

"Grape," she said.

JOKES FOR WOMEN ONLY'S

ASTROLOGICAL GUIDE TO MEN

USE THIS HANDY GUIDE TO FIND YOUR IDEAL MATE.....

AQUARIUS (Jan. 20 - Feb. 18)

The Aquarius man has an inventive mind and is inclined to be progressive. They lie a great deal. They are also inclined to be careless and impractical, causing them to make the same mistakes repeatedly. Everyone thinks they are fucking jerks.

PISCES (Feb. 19 - Mar. 20)

Pisces men have vivid imaginations and often think they are being followed by the FBI or the CIA. They have minor influence over their friends and people resent them for flaunting their power. Pisces men lack confidence and are generally cowards. They have a tendency to screw small animals and pick their nose a lot.

AIRES (Mar. 21 - Apr. 19)

Aires men are the pioneer type and hold most people in contempt. They are quick tempered, inpatient, and scornful of advice. They are pricks.

TAURUS (Apr. 20 - May 20)

The Taurus male is a practical and persistent person. He has a dogged determination and works like hell. Most people think they are stubborn and bullheaded. They are nothing but goddamn communists.

GEMINI *(May 21 - June 20)*

The Gemini man is a quick and intelligent thinker. People like them because they are bisexual. However, they are inclined to expect too much for too little. This means that they are cheap bastards. They are notorious for thriving on incest.

CANCER *(June 21 - July 22)*

Cancer men are sympathetic and understanding to other people's problems. People think he is a sucker. They are always putting things off. That is why they will always be on welfare and won't be worth a shit.

LEO (July 23 - Aug. 22)

Leo considers himself a born leader. Others think he is pushy. Most Leos are bullys. They are vain and can't tolerate honest criticism. Their arrogance is disgusting. Leo men are thieving bastards and kiss mirrors alot.

VIRGO (Aug. 23 - Sept. 22)

The Virgo man is the logical type and hates disorder. This shit-picking is sickening to his friends. He is cold and unemotional and often falls asleep while screwing. Virgos make good bus drivers and pimps.

LIBRA *(Sept. 23 - Oct. 22)*

Libra men tend to be the artistic type and have a difficult time with reality. Most Libra men are gay, but their chances for employment and monetary gain are excellent. All Libra's die of some form of venereal disease.

SCORPIO *(Oct. 23 - Nov. 21)*

Scorpio men are shrewd in business and can't be trusted. They shall achieve the pinnacle of success because of their total lack of ethics. They are perfect sons-of-bitches. Most Scorpios are murdered.

SAGITTARIUS (Nov. 22 - Dec. 21)

Sagittarius men are optimistic and enthusiastic. They have a reckless tendency to rely on luck since they have no talent. The majority of Sagittarians are either drunks or pot heads. People laugh at them alot because they are always getting fucked.

CAPRICORN (Dec. 22 - Jan. 19)

Capricorn men are conservative and afraid of taking risks. They are basically chicken-shit. There has never been a Capricorn of any importance. They should kill themselves.

All in all, I don't want you to get the impression from this book that MEN are all bad. They are a pain and they do irritating things like leave the toilet seat up, but there are compensations.....

I just can't think of any right now......

Do you know any good
"JOKES FOR WOMEN ONLY?"

If so, send them to:
P.O. Box 26451
Columbus, Ohio 43226

There can be no compensation, (Sorry!)
But the truely great ones will be
immortalized in print!

Thank you,

Susan Savannah